THE FLYING HAMMER

The Flying Hammer

An Insider's Collection of Saleroom Howlers

IAIN GALE

Illustrations by
George Gale

ELM TREE BOOKS LONDON

First published in Great Britain 1985
by Elm Tree Books/Hamish Hamilton Ltd
Garden House 57-59 Long Acre London WC2E 9JZ

British Library Cataloguing in Publication Data

Gale, Iain
The flying hammer: an insider's collection
of saleroom howlers.
1. Art auctions
I. Title
380.1′457 N8602

ISBN 0-241-11578-7

Filmset by Pioneer
Printed in Great Britain by
Billings, Worcester

To Richard

Contents

Acknowledgements

I should like to thank all those at Christie's Scotland, in particular Dermot Chichester, Denis Hillier, Jolyon Hudson, Jackie Lacey, Neil Macrae, Edward Monagle, Araminta Ritchie, Andy Taylor, and Bernard 'Flanagan' Williams. Also Helen Bassett (for typing my atrociously indecipherable manuscript), British Rail Scotland (for *all* those useful delays), Christie's, Christie's South Kensington, Janet Dunbar, Sotheby's, Sotheby's Glasgow, and, of course, my parents.

Introduction

Glancing at the saleroom page of a daily paper, the casual reader cannot fail to be struck by the enormous sums anonymous collectors pay for a single picture, piece of furniture or work of art. To the layman this row of figures might seem an extortionate amount to pay for one item. 'Money for old rope' he says, before quietly slipping away to the attic, in the hope of uncovering some long neglected family heirloom of unprecedented worth. Clutching his potential fortune, he will then hurry off to have it valued, thus taking his first steps into the complex world of the auction houses.

To the majority of clients this world for ever remains a mystery. Such is the discretion of the charming young lady at the front counter and the nonchalance of the smooth-tongued expert, that by the time the piece has been sold the owner will have no less vague an understanding of the workings of these curious establishments than he had before.

The intricate mechanics of the saleroom are a closely guarded secret and it is only occasionally that a blunder proves so disastrous that it is seized upon by the press and captures the public's imagination. Only then does the truth emerge — that behind the polished veneer of long established respectability lies a carefully concealed abundance of notable (and legendary) howlers.

The Luck of the Auction

I hold that no man upon town can be said to have completed his education unless he has taken a course of auctions

'Nemo', in City Press, *April 1875*

Our exploration of the lighter side of the auction world starts with a few cautionary tales for prospective clients and takes us back to Ancient Rome and what is probably the earliest auction on record. The word 'auction' is derived from the Latin 'auctio', meaning 'Increase' and the first auctions are believed to be those held on the fields of battle to divide the spoils of war. On 28 March 193 A.D., the 12,000-strong Praetorian Imperial Guard extended the practice when they decided to depose the Emperor, Pertinax, after a reign of only eighty-six days. Having beheaded him, they rushed to the ramparts of their camp with the bloody trophy and declared the Empire for sale to the highest bidder. Competition for 'the purple' soon narrowed itself down to two prospective candidates — Sulpicianus, father-in-law of the murdered Emperor (who had, in fact, probably masterminded the coup), and a wealthy and foolish Senator named Didius Julianus. After fierce bidding Sulpicianus dropped out and the Empire was 'knocked down' to Julianus for 300 million sesterces. Julianus, however, had even less time than his predecessor to enjoy his new exalted position. The military governors of three provinces immediately revolted and he was beheaded by General Septimus Severus of Parnonia only twenty-two days after having settled his account.

The Emperor Julianus was only the first of a long line of successful bidders who have been unable to appreciate the prizes they have won at auction. Recently, a private performance by the popular female

LOT XII
J. SILVANUS
AUCTIONEERS

contemporary dance group Pan's People was put up for auction at Sotheby's on behalf of charity. The lot was announced, the girls appeared before the rostrum to give a brief taste of what might be won, and went into a fast moving, hip-grinding routine, guaranteed to inflame many a prospective buyer. They were eventually knocked down, for a considerable sum, to an old and wealthy businessman. However, this aged dance enthusiast, presumably from sheer over anticipation, passed away before he had had time to view the performance for which he had paid.

Another equally unfortunate buyer was Stanislas II of Poland. Stanislas wished to furnish Poland with a National Gallery and for this purpose commissioned the art dealer and critic Noel-Joseph Desanfans, who was also his consul to the Court of St James, to purchase the finest of the pictures being sent for sale in London by the terrified French nobility during the turbulent pre-Revolutionary period. Carrying out his task with great efficiency, Desanfans secured, among other pictures, Claude's marvellous 'St Ursula and her maidens', and Holbein's cartoon for his painting of Henry VIII granting his charter to the Surgeon-Barber's company, which was much admired a century before by Samuel Pepys.

There was, however, one small problem for Stanislas. Much to his annoyance, both Russia and Prussia decided to invade his kingdom, and set about dividing it between themselves with their customary ruthlessness. The ill-fated Stanislas was deposed and a 'National' Gallery was out of the question in a nation no longer on the map. Desanfans was not paid and was forced to consign the magnificent collection to Mr Christie who, in April 1786, was only too pleased to dispatch it with his usual flair.

The period of the French Revolution saw a boom in the London auction market. Looking through the catalogues of that period one is constantly struck by references to 'the property of many emigrant noblemen' — a euphemism for the impoverished French aristocrats forced to sell their treasured possessions. Among the many fine collections consigned for sale to London by French noble families who unfortunately were unable to follow them, was the fabulous collection of jewels, sold in 1795, belonging to the beautiful Madame du Barry, mistress of Louis XV. Despite having managed to escape from France with many of her valuables, she could not bear the thought of being parted from those she had been forced to leave behind. On returning to retrieve them she fell into the hands of the revolutionaries and went under the guillotine in the same year.

Perhaps the collection with the most ill-fated provenance to reach the London art market during this period was that of the condemned Duc d'Orleans, which was sold at Christie's in 1798. This was an important group of pictures including Correggio's *Leda*, Poussin's *Seven Sacraments,* the great Bridgewater Titians, and major works by Raphael and Velazquez. The pictures had all previously been sold by Orleans to a Belgian banker, a shrewd entrepreneur who cleverly passed them on to a collector. The collector rapidly set about the construction of a great gallery in which to exhibit them, but this enterprise was curtailed by the Revolution. The collector then successfully transported the pictures to London, but he himself missed the boat, was captured by the Revolutionary authorities while making his escape, and followed in the footsteps of the previous owner of the paintings to the infamous Place de la Guillotine.

Within their walls, auction houses carry countless tales of ruin and destitution, but not all are quite so romantic as those of the French Revolution. Frank Bowen's Soho auction room sells office furniture, household effects, and liquidated property. In a sale there in the mid-1970s a few lots came up, poignantly referred to in the catalogue as being sold 'By order of the trustees R.t.e. P.L.M., deceased in bankruptcy'. Clues to the cause of this bankruptcy were to be found in the lots themselves, among which were thirteen suits and nineteen pairs of shoes as well as golf and cricket trophies. Thanks to the discretion of the considerate cataloguer, the full identity of 'P.L.M.' was withheld. This thoughtfulness, however, was rendered worthless on examination of the trophies, all of which were proudly engraved with the bankrupt's full name.

Art and Entertainment

We know that the tail must wag the dog, for the horse is drawn by the cart, but the Devil whoops, as he whooped of old: 'It's clever, but is it art?'

Rudyard Kipling,
The Conundrum of the Workshops

The saleroom, the opinion of experts, and the values which they place on pictures have been a major influence on public taste since the eighteenth century. Nowadays contemporary abstract works by Frank Stella and Jackson Pollock sell in London and New York for hundreds of thousands of pounds, but the art-buying public has not always been so adventurous in its choice, often resulting in what to us seems a painfully obvious lack of foresight.

Sir John Everett Millais, leading light of the Pre-Raphaelite movement, who, after his marriage, like so many artists, lost his true conviction and turned to painting 'pretty pictures', was the most highly paid painter of his day when selling direct to clients, but this popularity did not stretch as far as the saleroom. In 1874 he sold privately to Bolckow, the Victorian iron baron, his famous work *The North-West Passage* for £4,930. However, when it was knocked down at Christie's in 1888 the highest bid was only £4,200. Millais' unpopularity was so great that the cheering from the crowd assembled outside on hearing this could be heard in King Street, and right along St James's. Bolckow's judgement was later vindicated, however. Millais' *Dropped from the Nest* was sold at Christie's in 1978 for £35,000.

The great J. M. W. Turner also had his share of opposition from contemporary critics, both in and out of the saleroom, inspiring the novelist Mark Twain to describe his painting *The Slave Ship* as:

> A tortoise-shell cat having a fit in a plate of tomatoes.

While the *Literary Gazette* of May 1842 suggested that his technique was accomplished:

> By throwing handfuls of white and blue and red at the canvas, and letting what would stick, stick.

It was, however, at the de Tabley sale at Christie's in 1827 that Turner, amidst the cheers of his spiteful contemporaries filling the saleroom, had to undergo the ultimate indignity of buying back one of his own paintings, *Sun Rising Through Vapour*. By the 1900s, however, Turner's work was well in vogue and was being so widely imitated that it merited the following caption to a cartoon by Gardy in *Punch*:

> Lot 52, a genuine Turner, painted during the artist's lifetime.

The art-buying public, it seems, had, once again, lacked foresight. Turner's *Folkestone* was sold at Sotheby's in 1984 for £6,700,000. A record price for any oil painting.

Possibly the most notorious art scandals of the Victorian era surround the American aesthete James Abbott McNeill Whistler. Following criticism from that doyen of the art world, John Ruskin, Whistler's pictures sold for ridiculously small sums in the sale-room: at the William Graham sale at Christie's in 1888 one of his atmospheric *Nocturnes* made only sixty guineas. An account states that:

> When this lot came up there was a slight attempt at an ironical cheer, which, being mistaken for serious applause, was instantly suppressed by an angry hiss.

Ruskin, being far too staunchly Victorian in his taste, did not anticipate the aesthetic revolution. A fairly minor work by Whistler was sold at Christie's in March 1983 for £42,000.

The great English Rococo artist William Hogarth was well known for his unorthodox views on art. He completely lost faith in the auction houses of the time and decided to strike out on his own, holding two sales at his house, The Golden Head, in Leicester Fields in January 1743 and April 1744.

For the first he produced a catalogue satirising the auction world. It was quite well attended and all the lots were sold, but its success was evidently due entirely to its curiosity value for at his second sale Hogarth had only *one* bidder, a Mr Lane of Hillingdon. Hogarth had banned all dealers from the sale, and despite his postponing for an hour (a practice unthinkable in any major auction house) was still left with only Mr Lane. It was Hogarth's detractors who lost out, however, as among the lone bidder's purchases was a *Portrait of the Jeffrey's family,* sold in 1981 at Sotheby's for £167,360.

Undeterred by this failure, Hogarth also attempted to liberate his fellow artists from the necessity of slavishly imitating the old masters — the only way often in which artists could make any money. He persuaded several of his young contemporaries to hold a sale themselves and designed a satirical catalogue. The sale was a disaster. The catalogue outsold the pictures. The artists made nothing, but a rather embarrassed Mr Hogarth collected £6,500.

Taste in art is conditioned by emotion, and only a man of the utmost coolness can detach himself from such prejudices. In the words of Oscar Wilde:

> It is only the auctioneer who can equally and impartially admire all schools of art.
>
> *The Critic as Artist,* 1891

Apart from its role as a centre of artistic interest, the auction house has been for centuries a centre of social activity. It is as much a part of the fashionable world as the theatre, charity balls, and 'the sport of Kings'. A marvellous parody of Christie's in the reign of William IV is to be found in *La Belle Assemblee*, the *Tatler* of the time:

> The staircase was so thickly thronged with Dukes, and Marquesses and Earls, old dowagers and young heiresses, dashing officers of the Tenth, venerable divines and Members of Parliament. There was my Lord So and So calling his Grace the Duke of Such and Such, and there was gallant Colonel Somebody, shaking hands with the Hon. Major Nobody, while old Lady Asterisk, with a fat poodle under her arm, which she would *not* resign, made way after her fair daughter, who was leaning on a gay Captain of the Guards. . . . The noble crowd broke into groups; there was a truce to the levelling of glasses, and the buzz and murmur — the 'beautiful!' 'superb!' 'unique!' 'unquestionable!' died away as the auctioneer mounted his rostrum.

Since the eighteenth century, and presumably since Roman times, the fashionable and scholarly have flocked to the public auction to be both amused and educated.

> From Loo she rises with the rising sun, and Christie's sees her aching head at one.

Gale

So runs a rhyme by the author of 'Town Eclogues', satirising the lifestyle of a fashionable young lady of the 1770s. The saleroom has always been the haunt of the cognoscenti. Benjamin Robert Haydon, the nineteenth-century historical painter (and tragic suicide), relates an amusing episode on visiting a view at Christie's in the 1800s, accompanied by his friend William Wordsworth:

> A copy of the Transfiguration was at the head of the room, and in the corner a beautiful copy of the *Cupid and Psyche* kissing. Cupid is taking her lovely chin, and turning her pouting mouth to meet his while he archly bends his own down as if saying 'Pretty dear!' You remember the exquisite group . . . ? Catching sight of Cupid, as he and I were coming out, Wordsworth's face reddened, he showed his teeth, and then said in a loud voice . . . 'The Devvvvvils!'

Saleroom entertainment was not just confined to artists and the upper echelons of society. In the Paris of the 1870s, there were a great many sales of Impressionist pictures, one of which took place on 24 March 1875 at the Hôtel Drouot. The passions of the French people, particularly the Parisians, are easily aroused, and the brightly coloured daubs of Monet and his contemporaries jarred with the conservative artistic tastes of their compatriots. One of the infamous Paris mobs soon gathered outside the saleroom, and assaulted the doors, eventually managing to burst in and attack the bidders, among whom was the great collector Victor Chouquet. Some of the protestors got as far as the rostrum and began to slash at the bright canvases while the auctioneer and his clerk looked on in horror. The gendarmerie were called and hastily formed a human cordon around the rostrum, gradually forcing the mob back into the street. The sale, of course, continued.

The Paris mob was obviously still artistically aware when, in July 1889, J. F. Millet's painting *L'Angelus* was put up for auction at the Galerie Sedelmeyer. At the view the experts and nobility were discreetly admitted by a door at the rear of the establishment in order that they might have a little time in which to examine the work before the general public arrived to view a painting which had come to be regarded as something of a National Monument.

Private views are frequent events in the art world, but there can never have been another like this. When the main doors were finally opened and the public admitted, they found that the hall was already full. Being good Republicans they refused to leave and very soon a riot broke out. The police arrived. Abuse was freely exchanged, arrests were made and gendarmes assaulted. Miraculously, however, the picture remained unharmed.

The sale itself proved to be just as eventful. Before long, two major bidders emerged — Georges Petit on behalf of the French nation on the one hand, and J. F. Sutton, the New York art dealer, on the other. The picture was eventually knocked down to La Republique for 104,000 francs. Or so it seemed, except that Sutton's man immediately stood up and protested that he had still been bidding. The room split into two factions and a full scale debate arose on the saleroom floor as to whether the picture should be allowed to leave France. Eventually the auctioneer managed to make himself heard above the uproar and the picture was sold, for 553,000 francs, to the French nation, amid enthusiastic shouts of patriotic subscription bids. The minister for the arts was immediately hailed as a national hero. The crowd searched him out in the turmoil of the saleroom, and, lifting him shoulder high, carried him through the streets of Paris.

But that was not the end of the matter. After the sale, most of the subscription bidders dropped out or 'disappeared'. The French Senate was unable to secure enough money to pay for the picture and was thus forced to let it go to Sutton. However, once in the United States, Sutton could not find a buyer for the picture and, rather than be lumbered with it, he sold it to a certain Monsieur Chauchard of Paris – at whose bequest it now hangs in the Louvre.

Nowadays, it is rare for the peace of the saleroom to be disturbed by anything other than a quiet murmur of surprise. A story is told, however, of the comedian George Robey, latterly an enthusiastic collector of fine Chinese porcelain. He was bidding at an auction in Puttick and Simpson's London auction rooms in 1927 when a model of a farmyard cock came up for sale. Robey, not one to miss an opportunity to perform, stood up, turned to the audience, and went into an enthusiastic impression of the animal, clucking wildly, flapping his arms and stamping his foot on the floor. He was received with polite applause, and once he had bowed and sat down, the sale was resumed as if nothing had happened.

Inhabitants of the Saleroom

All professions are conspiracies

George Bernard Shaw

The public image of the staff of a smart saleroom is of a combination of haughty auctioneers, curiously effete experts, chinless young upper-class twits, 'Sloane Rangers', and stalwart Cockney porters. Although like many generalisations this is based on a certain amount of truth, it is largely a fallacious caricature.

Each of these 'types' is prone to everyday mistakes and in a profession which prides itself on perfection such occurrences are never allowed to pass unnoticed.

i. Auctioneers and other Experts

The man who is stationed at the door does not pick people's pockets, that is done by the auctioneer.

Samuel Johnson, Boswell, *8 May 1775*

The man who proclaims with a hammer that he has picked a pocket with his tongue.

Ambrose Bierce, 'The Auctioneer',
The Devil's Dictionary, *1906*

The auctioneer is the figure in the public eye. Although he is often the leading expert in his particular department, he does not usually conform to the traditional image of an expert — that of a greying old man locked away with other people's treasures in some remote corner of a dusty room. Instead, he is at the forefront of the sale. It is his responsibility as to whether the work of the other experts has been worthwhile, and it is probably this pressure which serves to explain his characteristically mercurial temperament and silvery tongue.

CATALOGUE

At a Saturday sale of books at Sotheby's in the 1890s taken by Tom Hodge, the only active partner at the time, a number of lots in succession were sold for only one or two shillings each. When the next lot came up, the book dealer Bertram Dobell, with characteristically impudent sarcasm, again bid only one shilling, even though it was a particularly fine illuminated manuscript.

'You ought to know better than that sir,' attacked Hodge.

'No,' replied Dobell, 'I'll give you a shilling for any lot sir.'

The manuscript eventually fetched over £1,000. As the sale progressed a few nondescript lots of books came up for which there were no bids. The hammer fell and Hodge announced:

'At a shilling to Mr Dobell.'

Dobell stood up and protested loudly that he had not been bidding to which Hodge replied:

'Just now you said you would give me a shilling for any lot.'

A long faced Mr Dobell ended the day making his way down the street with a wheelbarrow laden with *all* of the unwanted lots.

Tom Hodge's ploy obviously didn't go unmarked. That well known figure of the world of antiques, Arthur

Negus, related how, at a sale of household goods at the West Country auctioneers Bruton Knowles, a rusty pram was offered. Norman Bruton, the auctioneer, was taken aback.

'Whatever's that?' he asked the porter.

'Lot 17 sir, perambulator sir' was the reply.

Bruton opened the bidding.

'Oh dear, who'll give me one shilling for it? If anyone looks at me I shall knock it down to them for a shilling.'

Immediately everyone in the room began to study their catalogue diligently. The auctioneer grew tired.

'I shall knock it down to whom I like for one shilling. Lady Gwyn Evans, one shilling.' Then added, with a smile, 'Just as well to be prepared, madam.' (Lady Gwyn Evans was then sixty-five.)

THE FLYING HAMMER

The auction-going public is well aware that the saleroom is the domain of the auctioneer, and regard him with justified apprehension, teetering on the edge of their chairs if, in the course of an auction he should pause, or be diverted from his immediate purpose.

The diarist Charles Dibdin describes George Leigh, partner of John Sotheby in the 1760s, as an intimidating tyrant:

> When a high-priced book is balanced between £15 and £20 it is a *fearful* sign of its reaching an additional sum if Mr Leigh should lay down his hammer and delve into his crumplehorn shaped snuff box.

The hammer is not always 'laid down with such care'. At a sale of stamps at Robson-Lowe's Pall Mall rooms in the 1950s the auctioneer was a certain lady notorious for demanding high standards of order in the saleroom. On this particular occasion she was repeatedly forced to ask a Dr Baker, a respected collector, to desist from conversing with his neighbour. He became silent for only a few moments and then began to talk once more. This went on with each request he was given, until eventually the lady auctioneer became so irritated she warned the good doctor that if he continued to speak she would have no compunction in throwing the hammer at him. He was silent. Five minutes later, however, this unfortunately verbose philatelist uttered just a single word and went down in auction history. The hammer flew through the air and dealt him a very hard and bloody blow on the nose.

Lady auctioneers are just as likely to encounter problems as their male counterparts. Nicola Redway of Sotheby's was taking one of her first sales of fine Art Nouveau collectables in Monte Carlo. One of the first lots to come up was an exquisite bronze and ivory sculpture group of half naked dancing girls in typically suggestive poses. The piece was not in the best condition and seemed to be a little loose on its marble base. In an attempt to raise a bid for the piece Miss Redway momentarily forgot its subject matter, and when announcing the lot commented:

'I believe that all they need is a screw.'

Thomas Woods of Christie's who is caricatured as the auctioneer, in Edwin Long's Victorian painting *The Babylonian Marriage Market*, enjoys the not entirely enviable reputation of having been the most temperamental, masterful and bigoted auctioneer of all time. When, in 1882, the representatives of the National Gallery were outbid by Sedelmeyer of Paris on a picture by the fifteenth-century Italian master Antonella da Messina, a work of which Woods was especially fond, he had no hesitation in publicly rebuking them with a spirited tirade from the rostrum.

Woods was also the auctioneer at the sale of the Doetsch collection of pictures at Christie's in 1895. It was his opinion that these pictures had undergone such restoration as to make the attributions given them almost worthless. Nevertheless, Christie's produced an important catalogue in which experts presented arguments for their correct attribution. According to A. C. R. Carter, art critic of the *Daily Telegraph,* Woods was seen at the view to have 'sniffed and snarled at the pictures', while at the sale he made his feelings on the matter even more obvious. After seventy-three of the 448 lots had been knocked down Woods obviously couldn't stand it any longer. He went very red, and called out to one of his porters. A ladder was brought in and he descended from the rostrum and walked out. The sale, subsequently continued by a junior, made only £12,970 — a fraction of the anticipated total.

Auctioneers are also just as likely to fall prey to the gremlins that plague ordinary mortals. In 1969 at Christie's first sale to be held in Australia, a rostrum was specially constructed 'on site'. The great day came and the auctioneer, who had been flown all the way from 'the old country', went to ascend the rostrum when he suddenly disappeared from view — in their excitement, the builders had forgotten to put in a floor.

Apart from experts in specialised fields, each saleroom usually employs a number of regional representatives. These gentlemen generally possess an overall knowledge of antiques which may, however, be a little lacking in detail. One such representative was recently taken on by a respected Scottish saleroom. Arriving there on the first visit from his country house on the west coast, he proudly bore with him a small engraved glass bowl and an elegant decorated vase. Unfortunately, as he entered he tripped and fell, dropping the bowl, but luckily managing to catch the vase. On finding the porcelain and glass expert, the representative explained what had happened, making much of his successful rescue of the 'beautiful vase'. Bending down to examine the fragments of the glass bowl the expert discovered it to be by Tiffany and worth around £2,000. The vase, it emerged, was a contemporary piece of Minton china — shop price a few pounds.

Very occasionally, an auctioneer makes a major mistake. When this happens, it is usually a gross oversight and totally inexplicable, but it is generally carried off with the greatest panache. In the early 1970s, for example, the leading furniture expert of a London-based auctioneers entered the saleroom, ascended the rostrum, opened his marked copy of the catalogue, and started the sale. As it progressed he was astonished at the outrageous prices being paid. It was only after several lots had passed that he realised that he was, in fact, in the wrong saleroom, taking a sale not of rather dull furniture but of rare and highly prized antiquarian books.

It is surprising that a certain Irish auctioneer did not find himself in the same predicament. In the 1970s Arthur 'Chubby' Williams, of Hamilton and Hamilton the Dublin auctioneers, had eventually been forced to succumb to the necessity of wearing spectacles. Ever conscious of his public image, however, he refused to wear them while on the rostrum. He was thus totally unable to focus clearly on either his catalogue or the very object he was to sell. His solution was to avail himself of the services of a porter who, when asked, would shout out the lot number and provide a full and yawningly lengthy description of each article as it came up for sale.

Auctioneers do not always confine their eccentric behaviour to the rostrum. As well as being the front man, the auctioneer is also, usually, the leading expert in a particular department. Christie's Oriental ceramics expert in the 1960s and 70s was renowned as a particularly hyperactive gentleman. Despite the powerful sedatives presented by his doctor he was famous for doing press-ups behind his office desk. On one occasion a certain porter had been rather cheeky and when the unfortunate young man passed by, he leapt out and attempted to strangle him from behind.

On another occasion this gentleman's secretary had so annoyed him that he picked up her typewriter and hurled it across the room at her. Happily he missed, and, Christie's secretaries being made of strong stuff, he soon found himself being paid back in kind.

Many people are swift to classify the pin-striped auctioneers as empty-headed chinless wonders whose pedigree is so exclusive that they do not have a brain between them. What many people may not realise is that even if these gentlemen may not have the highest academic qualifications, they do have 'connections', and in the art market that, or the lack of it, can still mean the difference between success and utter failure.

Perhaps the best example of this system in action is provided by the sale of a picture through a provincial branch of a highly respected auction house in the early 1980s. The painting, a superb example of the work of a pupil of Edmund Bristow, the eighteenth-century English sporting artist, had hung for many years on the damask-covered wall of a great baronial mansion. It depicted a covey of grouse at daybreak and apart from its characteristically naive charm, was remarkable for its excellent condition.

Before being offered for sale the picture was well catalogued, and catalogues, as always, went out to subscribers and prospective clients. The director of the picture department was, however, rather more concerned with his own self-glorification than the business in hand, and, being something of a social climber with only one foot on the first rung, failed to circulate the catalogue among the local landed gentry, where most of the interest would have been, preferring to send it to bosses of industry, local entrepreneurs and other such gentlemen of his acquaintance. Not surprisingly, the picture was unsold at half the estimate of £1,000 to £2,000.

Several months later the director went a little too far and found himself out of a job. His replacement was an auctioneer of the old school who discovered, among his legacies, this fine sporting picture. By the time the new director encountered the painting, however, it was barely recognisable. So negligent had his predecessor been that the surface was covered in scratches and the canvas torn in several places. It appeared, however, that the picture would have to be sold, and after having had it repaired, the new director set about circulating a catalogue. The number of interested parties was quadrupled, and the picture made £9,700.

On several occasions an important sale has only been concluded because of the eagle eyes of the experts. A Sotheby's picture expert in New York who also happened to be a first rate pianist, once paid an informal visit to a friend of a friend who owned a piano which she was anxious to have repaired. He advised her, rather sadly, that the instrument was beyond repair and told her to buy another. She was most upset, explaining to the young man that being a widow she could not possibly afford one. As he was leaving, the young gentleman happened to notice a couple of pictures leaning against the wall. With the expert's typical inquisitiveness he asked what they might be.

'Oh those,' said the woman, 'they're just some rubbish that my late husband wasted his money on years ago.'

Curiosity got the better of the Sotheby man who, bending down to look at a canvas, immediately realised that they could be of some interest. They were, in fact, a Gauguin and a Cezanne, and when auctioned in New York realised more than $1,000,000 between them.

It is not uncommon for people to have in their possession articles worth a great deal more than they imagine. A woman once took a picture into Sotheby's in Bond Street and asked those at reception whether they would buy it from her for £100 as she was desperate to raise the deposit for a car. She was most upset when told that they did not actually *purchase* pictures, but that they would be quite happy to put it up for auction. Reluctantly the woman agreed. An expert was summoned and the picture appraised. The painting in question was found to be a rare depiction of the 'Temptation of Eve' by the German sixteenth-century artist Hans Baldung Grien, and was eventually sold for £249,000. (No doubt the owner was then able to afford a slightly more expensive vehicle.)

It is just as usual for people to overvalue something, and on such occasions working at reception, or on the 'front counter', demands a good deal of charm, discretion, and, at times, great ingenuity.

The head of Sotheby's furniture department was once at the front counter examining an Edwardian bureau. The owner believed it to be of immense value and attempted, with mounting indignation, to explain to the expert its true worth. He eventually exploded with rage and threatened in future to take all of his business to Christie's. The expert's reply was characteristically pointed but at the same time faultlessly courteous.

'Sir, I can recommend our esteemed rivals to you with the clearest conscience, and fortunately for my conscience, they are unlikely to ask whether I can recommend you to them.'

At a well attended antiques roadshow held by Christie's Scotland at Scone near Perth, their porcelain expert found himself faced, among other things, with a tiny Chinese bowl. Having examined this item carefully, he apologetically told the owner that it was a piece of modern export porcelain, a copy of a fine sixteenth-century bowl, and thus not worth more than

a few pounds. The owner, who turned out to be the president of Scone Antiques Society, was furious. He informed the expert that he was wrong, and that he knew the piece was the genuine article because he had taken it to the local Chinese restaurant and had them decipher the date on the base. He stormed out in disgust, leaving the expert somewhat embarrassed, but none the less firm in his opinion.

Later the same day the expert caught sight of the same difficult client engaged in an animated conversation with a colleague from the silver department. On eavesdropping, he discovered the topic of discussion to be a small silver dish which the owner insisted was ancient Persian, and his colleague maintained was modern Spanish. Seeing that neither of the protagonists was about to step down, the porcelain expert intervened, and addressing the furious owner, said:

'It is indeed fortunate for us, sir, that to the best of my knowledge the town of Scone does not yet possess a Persian restaurant.'

The expert is not infallible, however, and can often become bigoted in his judgements. In the early 1980s, for example, a leading auction house conducted a valuation of the contents of the family home of a Scottish landed gentleman. Among the inventory appeared a large painting of a Venetian scene — *The Piazza San Marco*; ascribed to a nineteenth-century Italian master. On the demise of the ancient landowner the picture, along with other items from the house, were consigned to the saleroom for auction. An expert examined the picture with great care, commenting on the brushwork, tone, colour and condition, and eventually cataloguing the work as 'Italian school, nineteenth-century'.

On the day of the sale the picture, which had been hanging on view in the saleroom for three days, happened to attract the attention of a young trainee cataloguer, fresh from University. He commented to the expert that it appeared to him to be very close to the work of the English Victorian artist Edward Pritchett.

'Pritchett?' poo-pooed the expert. 'Nonsense', and stormed off in a glorious huff.

The sale was well attended by the picture trade, but bidding was slow and when the Venetian view came up it was knocked down for only £800, against an estimate of £1,000 to £2,000. The landowner's beneficiaries were most disappointed, having always considered the picture to have been worth a great deal more. Disappointment turned to fury, however, when, two months later, the old man's granddaughter, glancing through a friend's copy of an auction catalogue, came across the picture, catalogued as 'Edward Pritchett — *Piazza San Marco*' with an estimate of £4,000 to £6,000. It had been sold on the previous afternoon to a respectable American dealer for £6,800.

Family traditions can pose considerable problems. An old-master painting expert was called down to the picture section of Sotheby's front counter to be faced by a Lady of noble bearing, burdened with a black and pitchy Dutch still life painting of flowers. She was of the opinion that due to its unquestionable provenance her picture must be a valuable masterpiece. The expert began by extolling its virtues. He pointed out the fine brushstrokes and carefully noticed the aesthetic purpose of the attention to detail. He put forward attributions — was it Van der Ast, or could it possibly be Bosschaert? He was eventually, however, forced to come to the point, and had to ask:

'But your Ladyship, which way up does it go?'

Again at Sotheby's, a book expert was once called to reception and asked to examine a large leather-bound tome.

'Do you realise, sir,' said the expert, knowingly, 'that this is a *Book of Hours*?'

'Indeed it is not, sir,' replied the horrified owner. 'I can assure you that it has been in *my* family for well over two hundred years!'

A young Sotheby's cataloguer in the 1970s developed his own special way of dealing with clients. Faced with a dark and dingy 'school' picture he surfaced from the basement, where he had taken the work for perusal, wearing a lampshade on his head, and explained to the client that he was unable to 'throw

any light' on the painting. On another occasion he arrived back at the counter with one half of a ping-pong ball over each eye and declared that he 'could not see anything at all in the picture'.

Deceased properties are frequently offered for sale at auction and can sometimes lead to awkward moments. One young auctioneer, a porcelain expert, recently visited a house to value for auction several interesting items belonging to a deceased Scottish gentleman. As a mark of respect, he was soberly dressed in black.

The door was opened by the deceased's wife, an old lady also clad in black, who showed the young man into the sitting room. She offered him tea and sandwiches and cake and biscuits, followed by more tea. Eventually, having sat in abject silence for over an hour, the young man ventured to ask when he might have a look at what he had come to see.

The old lady nodded solemnly and leading the auctioneer through the house to a small door at the rear ushered him into a darkened room. When his eyes became accustomed to the light, he found himself confronted with a corpse propped up in a four poster bed, its eyes fixed in a wide-eyed stare.

'If you don't mind me saying so dear,' whispered the old lady, 'you're awful young for an undertaker.'

Experts are, as a breed, involved in a timeless love affair with their individual subjects. A prime example of this occurred in 1939 when Sotheby's Belgravia salerooms were gutted by fire. The blaze was fought to the last by a staunch team made up mainly of technical experts, led by Tim Clarke who later became a senior director. When he returned to the scene of the disaster the next morning, he was greeted by the sight of three of his book expert 'firemen' sitting amidst the smouldering debris reading an ancient copy of the unexpurgated version of *The Arabian Nights*!

This thirst for knowledge does not prevent experts from indulging their whimsical sense of humour. Brian Sewell, art critic of the *Tatler*, who once worked for Christie's, admits to two slightly fallacious catalogue entries. He had been considering thc attribution of a certain picture for quite some time when another cataloguer approached him and asked whether he had yet found an artist for the work. 'No,' replied Sewell, 'it's a right bastard.' The catalogue entry subsequently read 'R. Bastard'.

Mr Sewell also admits to having been responsible for the creation of that accomplished Dutch seventeenth-century master Herts van Rental.

Brian Sewell is not alone in 'creating' artists. One of the most common attributions given to the many nineteenth-century English pastoral landscapes which all auction houses receive for sale is 'Barker of Bath'. Thomas Barker of Bath (1769-1847) was a member of the 'indefatigable family of Barkers of Bath' of whom many were painters. A mischievous member of one team of London cataloguers became so incensed by the tedious regularity of this attribution that he decided on a slight whimsical variation — the picture concerned making it through to proof stage as 'Barker of Basildon'.

International auction houses suffer a variation of this problem when translating their catalogues, but usually the mistakes are unintentional. In Dutch, for instance, there is but one letter difference between certain words. For example, the word for 'advise' is spelt *raad* and the word for 'rape' *raap*. A well-known auction house was horrified to learn that the footnote of several translated copies of their catalogues ran as follows:

'Our experienced valuers will be pleased to rape you on any article.'

It is unlikely that any such attributions would have been passed by G. D. Hobson, a Sotheby's partner in 1909, who bore the nickname 'Il Magnifico'. Although he did not take sales, due to his acute deafness, Hobson always proof-read the catalogue carefully. His eye, however, was attuned to the academic, rather than mistakes of a more basic nature. On one occasion, while accompanying an important

BEWARE OF THE DOG

client around the view of a picture sale, Hobson was faced with a large oil portrait of a child standing beside a table, on which was a large conical hat. Glancing at the catalogue entry both he and the client noticed with amazement that the picture was described as 'Boy with a Dog'. The client asked the obvious question, where was the dog? 'Under the hat, I presume' was Hobson's reply.

A similar embarrassment occurred at Sotheby's first sale of Contemporary Art in December 1974. A composition entitled *Loop*, by the artist Elsworth Kelly, was held up by one of the porters. Immediately there were cries from the front row of the audience, who were diligently studying the photograph in their catalogues. Surely it was the wrong way up?

The auctioneer was forced to correct them.

'Believe it or not, Ladies and Gentlemen, Sotheby's catalogue is at fault.'

An auctioneer has to be prepared for many reactions from the audience. At a sale of Japanese artefacts in November 1967 John Harding, an expert on Japanese works of art, held up a superb Fachi sword blade made by the Japanese thirteenth-century swordsmith Masamune. He was surprised to see a besuited gentleman among the audience stand up and bow in his direction and then resume his seat. It turned out that the gentleman was simply indulging in the ancient Japanese custom of showing respect for a fine blade.

Occasionally even the most experienced and unflappable auctioneers can be left speechless.

Following the devastating Florentine floods of 1968, a group of philanthropic American ladies, the 'Women's Rehabilitation Committee', persuaded Sotheby's to attempt to obtain a picture from Picasso to be sold in aid of those made homeless on NBC television. The late Peter Wilson, Sotheby's indefatigable chairman, flew to Picasso's villa in the South of France, met the legendary artist, and was able to secure a work for the sale.

In the course of the eventually fruitful conversation, Wilson happened to mention a story he had heard about Picasso's pet parrot, which had apparently once eaten one of Picasso's pictures.

'Yes indeed,' affirmed Picasso. 'That is quite true.'

'What became of the parrot?' enquired Wilson politely.

'The parrot?' said Picasso. 'Oh, he died. The picture was his portrait.'

One should not leave the subject of the auctioneer with the misconception that he is totally cold and unfeeling. He does possess a degree of understanding for the public's sensitivity as was shown at the Chauncey Brothers' sale at Christie's in March 1770.

Lot 58 was described as:

> Albert Durer: an emblematical female figure curious.

However, that there was more to it than this is revealed in a manuscript note in the margin of one of the catalogues:

> 58. This was a naked female and the Auctioneer gave it the name of 'A Capital piece of Natural History' and it was held up with the wrong side toward the Company so as to be seen only by those who chose to go near and take it into their hands.

And sometimes the coolness of the auctioneer deserts him completely, as happened at Sotheby's sale of contemporary art in December 1974. When Lot 31 was announced, the porter held up, in his gloved hand, a small can inscribed in three languages:

> Produced by Piero Manzoni, Artist's Shit.

The auctioneer gently pulled a handkerchief from his breast pocket, held it to his nose, and sniffed. Unfortunately, he caught the eye of a friend in the audience and collapsed in a fit of helpless giggles, in which he was soon joined by the rest of the saleroom. The work of art failed to sell.

ii Porters

The man who by his labour gets his bread, in independent state.

Prior, The Old Gentry

Porters are a race apart. They work within a strict and time-honoured hierarchy and are united in the belief that experts are people needing to be humoured. Theirs is a world of strange customs and unspoken traditions. At Sotheby's in the nineteenth century most of the porters came from the Guards Employment Bureau and the names by which they referred to each other were mostly carried over from their army days. As late as the 1920s, the foreman porter, a Mr Carpenter, was known to his juniors as 'Corp'.

According to one source the porters at Sotheby's were always renowned for being in a perpetual state of drunkenness. The foreman porter in 1916 was a certain Mr James, who, when Lady Astor's Bill limiting drinking hours within public houses was passed, was heard to remark that this would at least mean that his men would be sober until 11 a.m.

In the late 1960s a porter was once inadvertently locked in the basement of a renowned London auction house for the duration of a weekend. No amount of appeals for help elicited any response, so being fairly well built he took himself off to the armoury store and, finding a halberd, hacked his way out of the basement and made his way through the building to the chairman's offices. The telephones were, of course, inoperative, and his search for food resulted only in a few dog-eared lunchtime sandwiches. He then suddenly had a brainwave. Remembering that a sale of wine was to be held the following week, he decided to liberate a few bottles and make the most of what promised to be a very dreary weekend. After a short search, he found what he was looking for. Case upon case of fine vintage

claret, hock, Burgundy, port, Madeira, sherry and champagne. The weekend passed surprisingly quickly. When faced with lack of food one can, by means of consolation, consume a quite amazing quantity of liquid. In the course of two days, the man consumed a total of thirty-four bottles, in his more sober moments keeping boredom at bay by reading books borrowed from the porcelain department, which he found most interesting.

On Monday morning, he was discovered by a wine expert, a bottle of sherry in his hand, seated on an Imari jardinière, perusing a work on *famille jaune* porcelain.

Needless to say, the unfortunate man lost his job. He did, however, go on to become an extremely well respected and successful dealer in Chinese porcelain.

Another porter from Sotheby's was once sent to a client who lived somewhere in the Midlands to pack some very valuable glass. On the morning of his arrival Sotheby's received an extremely irate telephone call from their client to say that the porter had arrived the worse for drink. Nothing they said could calm the client down, so the foreman was sent for to see if he could placate him. He told him that this particular porter was always safer and more efficient in his packing when drunk and that he should be allowed to get on with his work. The client reluctantly agreed and sure enough the glass arrived at New Bond Street perfectly packed and unbroken.

Sometimes the client, purchaser or vendor, is not quite so fortunate. A picture collected by its successful purchaser from a major London auction house was found to have had its frame badly damaged. The client was furious and it took a great deal of sweet-talking to calm him down. The picture was left at the warehouse to be restored and after a couple of weeks the client returned to collect it. Imagine his anger on finding that the picture was now in completely the wrong frame. A director was rushed to the scene and he attempted to mollify the unfortunate gentleman, agreeing that the firm would now deliver the picture, restored to its original frame, to his house in Wiltshire. The ill-starred painting was duly dispatched on a company van which, true to the best British traditions, broke down. The driver, a conscientious fellow, was careful to take the picture with him when he went to telephone the AA, who soon arrived and rescued him. It was only when he was half way to the nearest service-station that the driver realised he had left the picture in the telephone box. On his return, it had gone.

Delivery is a constant problem. At the sale of the contents of North Mimm's Park in 1978, a large brass bedstead was among the lots. When the buyer of the bed arrived to collect his purchase he was informed by a security guard that the porters were attempting to remove it from the bedroom. This, unfortunately, was located up a spiral staircase down which it soon became obvious the bed did not want to go. The purchaser, worried by the grunts and shouts he heard coming from above managed to slip past the security man and on reaching the top of the stairs was met with a bedroom full of porters, but no bed. The porters had exercised their traditional ingenuity. The gentleman looked out of the window and saw it half buried in the nearest rose bed.

When their own van was elsewhere, Christie's in Glasgow used to employ a contractor to remove contents from houses. This colourful gentleman was regrettably not as considerate to furniture as his full-time counterparts and over the years had developed quite a reputation for damaging the items which he brought in. He was a man of limited intelligence but great imagination which reached its peak when he removed some items of antique furniture from a deserted house in Glasgow. The furniture had been in perfect condition when seen by Christie's furniture expert. On arrival at the saleroom, however, it was found to be covered in scratches. When asked how this had happened, the slapdash removal man replied that the windows of the old house had been left open and that the hundreds of squirrels that inhabited the garden had come in and run around on the furniture, scratching it almost beyond repair. His services were not required again.

Porters are often faced with unforeseen and sometimes rather weird problems when unpacking items which arrive for sale. At Edmiston's of Glasgow, a chamber pot was once received from a deceased person's executry. The incredible stench which emitted from it was, on opening, found to be coming from a long-dead cat mummified inside a plastic bag.

Henry Stevens' nineteenth-century salerooms in King Street St James's specialised in the sale of strange objects. On one occasion in the 1860s Mr Stevens was most insistent that his foreman porter should inform him immediately when a rare Aye Aye (African squirrel) arrived from Madagascar. The great day eventually dawned, but Stevens found himself approached by a shadow of his former foreman, his face green, his arms trembling, almost in a faint. The Aye Aye (deceased) had been packed in a chemical solution, which in the course of the long journey had 'gone off'. The smell was unbearable.

There was an infamous occasion at a well established London auction house in the 1970s when a large quantity of bookcases arrived for sale all at the same time. Several porters had the unenviable task of transporting these up the main staircase. They succeeded in carrying the bases up the stairs, and arranging them carefully around the stairwell. However, their problems started with the bookcase tops. Managing, with great effort, to carry the first of these to the top of the stairs, they carefully put it down in order to take a 'breather'. While they were busy wiping their glistening brows, the cumbersome piece of furniture slowly edged its way towards the stairs and a gentle slide was followed by a head-over-heels tumble as it crashed into the entrance hall, narrowly missing several ladies and an elderly gentleman ascending the stairs to view the sale. The porters, looking rather sheepish, quickly gathered up the remains and went to get bookcase number two. This time they were slightly more successful, managing to raise the top on to its base beside the high bannister. The need for a rest once again intervened, but before they had had time to secure the top to base, it had leapt over the edge and crashed into splinters on the stairs below. Another narrow escape for the public, who were now rather gingerly ascending to view. As the third attempt met with early disaster, the air is said to have turned blue with expletives.

A porter at Sotheby's was discovered unpacking one of the items to be sold in their first ever sale of Contemporary Art in July 1973. It seemed to be a complicated parcel covered in sacking and tied with thick rope in strange and curious knots. An expert wearing a look of alarm rushed up to him and was only just in time to prevent the complete destruction of Christo's conceptual work *Wrapped Stand*.

Another Sotheby's porter was busily unwrapping a painting for the same sale when he recoiled in horror. The canvas had a large hole right through it. Quickly he rushed upstairs brandishing the receipt for the picture, on which he had carefully written 'damaged on arrival'. It was not until the damage had been examined by a picture expert that it was realised that the work had been deliberately defaced by its creator in order to convey his artistic message.

Porters love to play pranks. Particularly when this means that they can 'put one over' on the auctioneer. One of the latter, renowned for his phenomenally tight purse, once joined three of his porters for a night on the tiles, it being one of the boys' birthday. As they travelled from pub to pub, getting steadily more drunk, the young auctioneer lived up to his reputation by managing not to pay for a single round. The next morning the young man was to take a sale. Bleary-eyed and thick-headed, he made it on to the rostrum and started. Despite his appalling hangover the sale appeared to proceed quite well. Then, just after lot 40, the young man, now suffering from extreme dehydration, took a long drink from the water glass which is always an essential part of the auctioneer's equipment. Suddenly he froze. His complexion turned bright red and stumbling from the rostrum he gestured to an elder colleague to take over and fled the room.

The porters had replaced his glass of water with neat tequilla.

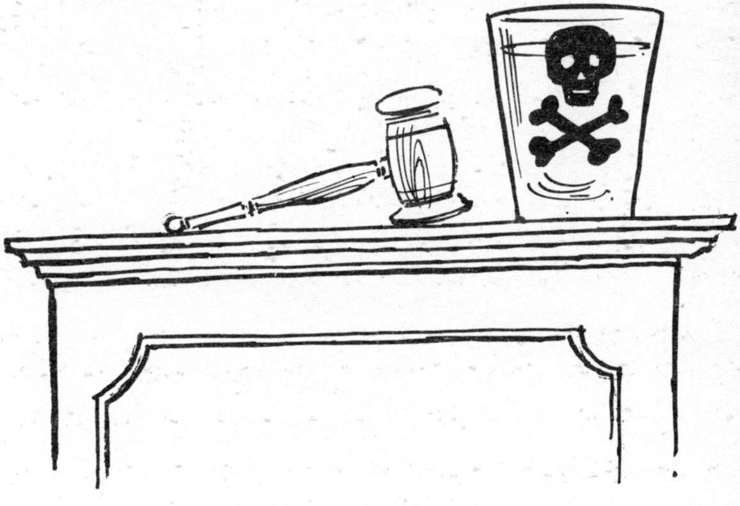

A porter at Sotheby's once decided to make a little extra money by accepting a dare from one of his colleagues. During the middle of an important furniture sale he leapt on top of a commode and went into a pelvis-rotating rendition, à la Elvis Presley, of the rock'n'roll classic 'Blue Suede Shoes'. He gave a complete performance, bowed gracefully, apologised to the stupefied audience, and descended. There was no encore.

A picture porter at Christie's in Glasgow, while hanging a particular sale for a three day public view, decided to use a little ingenuity and placed at the doorway, as the first exhibit to meet the public, a large bright yellow canvas by the Contemporary Scottish artist, Donald Bain of which the subject was an interior with an obese nude woman beating a cow.

iii Dealers

An auction is a publick sale
that injures those who fairly deal

(Egbert van Heemskerck II)

We now move on to the dealers, who certainly take their auction going with the utmost seriousness, even if they do not all subscribe to the advice given to their nineteenth-century counterparts by Champfleury:

> A plain overcoat without furs or trimming is the dress most propitious for making a good strike. To let yourself be carried away by the tide of bidding is to expect to make your fortune at roulette. Don't irritate your stomach by spicy meals, a bar of chocolate, or any sweet fortifies the system around four o'clock when the bidding gets hot. A bottle of smelling salts is indispensable to combat the exhaltations of the crowd.
>
> With this you will have a full life . . .

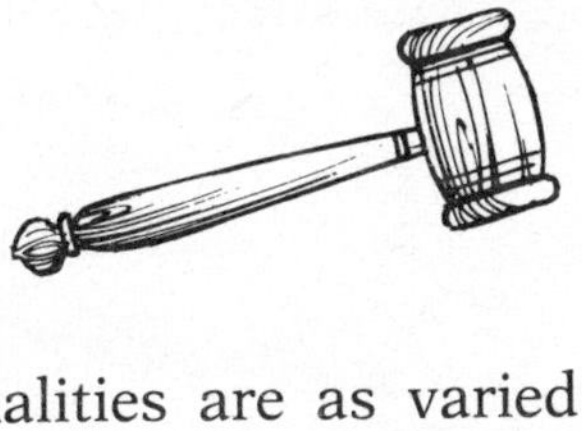

Dealers' personalities are as varied as the fields in which they specialise. They can be the most courteous of men, or they can be extremely fickle and even violent.

At the sale in the late nineteenth century of the contents of Tetten Hall near Wolverhampton, the seat of the Davenport family, an extraordinary row broke out between the London antique dealer Robert Partridge and his bidding partner for the day Morris Jacobsen. The famous dealer Joseph Duveen was wandering into the marquee during the interval when he was suddenly sent flying by Robert Partridge who was hurrying away from Morris Jacobsen clutching 'a parcel of showy cutlery', which, he claimed, was his share of their joint purchases. Jacobsen was making ground on Partridge, so he threw the package into the branches of a tree where it hung by a weighted piece of string, and made his escape. Jacobsen, unable to reach it, became incensed. Grabbing two bags of flour from the basket of a passing errand boy, Jacobsen sprinted after his erstwhile partner. He took aim and hurled the bags, the first of which dealt Partridge a hefty blow on the back of the neck. The second, however, caught Duveen full in the chest, and covered him with a fine white dust which it took the two dealers the rest of the day to wash off.

Joseph Duveen was also involved in an accident at a sale in Bootle. Just as he bent down to examine a dirt covered painting on panel, the crowd were taken with a great event on the rostrum and suddenly moved backwards, one gentleman knocking Duveen's head against the panel, which split in two. The auctioneer quickly noticed this, and as the panel happened by chance to be the next lot, bullied Duveen into bidding for it. The picture was sold to him for £1. When he got it home, Duveen found that his suspicions had been correct. The panel was an early work by Frans Hals, which he then sold on for £2,000.

Occasionally the auctioneer's ruthless nature backfires on him. A split panel does not necessarily mean a decrease in its value. One of the lots offered in one particular sale of Old Master pictures in London in the mid 1970s was a Flemish fifteenth-century painting on panel which, when its turn came, was held out in front of the auctioneer by the porter. The bidding was quite slow at first and the auctioneer was hard put to draw bids from the audience. Suddenly disaster struck. Perhaps the porter, slightly tired by this stage of the proceeding, applied pressure where it should not have been placed. Perhaps the spirit of the panel itself decided that self-destruction was the only answer to being scorned by the buying public. Whatever the cause, the effect was immediately obvious. The panel cracked, not from side to side but lengthways. The words with which the quick-witted auctioneer resurrected the sale are now legendary:

'Now ladies and gentleman, a bargain — two for the price of one!'

eventually selling the two pieces of panel for a not inconsiderable sum.

A story is often told about the Jewish dealer Willie De Freece. This gentleman aroused much comment by wearing a large gold ring inset with a single diamond on the third finger of his left hand. He had once seen an advertisement for a furniture auction only twenty minutes from London, at which he thought he might make a killing. However, it was to be held on a Saturday, the Jewish Sabbath. After great consideration De Freece succumbed to heathen temptation and attended the sale where he purchased for only a few pounds an extremely fine French inlaid commode, later selling it to a London dealer for £250. His guilty conscience for having bought it on the Sabbath did not allow him to put the money back into his business, so De Freece went out and invested it in the ring. Henceforth, whenever he was asked the story behind it, he would reply:

'I found it in a chest of drawers.'

A rather unsavoury aspect of the auction world is the Ring. This is a long established, and not strictly legal, convention by which a number of dealers get together before a sale and agree not to bid against one another on particular items, thus keeping the prices artificially low. After the sale the treasure trove of undersold lots is 'knocked out privately' among the participants, who are thus able to increase their profit margins considerably.

One house sale in the early 1980s took place at the ancestral home of a highland gentleman who was himself a noted auction-goer. Knowing the workings of 'the trade' he went to great pains to ensure that any ring of dealers which might be in operation on the day would not hold their 'knock out' anywhere on his land. On the great day he posted retainers, friends and saleroom porters at key positions about the estate and, sure enough, soon after the auction a group of carpet dealers were to be seen wandering around weighed down by numerous burdens. From the refreshment tent they were forced into the cook's pantry, and thence to the great hall itself. It was of no use. Nowhere were they able to find a secluded spot at which to divide their booty.

Sometime later in the afternoon, a vigilant porter on duty in the entrance hall was surprised by a commotion from the car park. On rushing outside he observed the group of carpet dealers cowering terrified beneath the fiery tirade of a furious young woman — the wife of the Managing Director of his firm of auctioneers. They had unwittingly chosen to 'knock out' their bargains on the bonnet of her husband's car.

The Bath dealer R. P. Way was on his way from the local station to a sale at a country house near Durston in Somerset when a terrific snow blizzard blew up. He was absolutely soaked, and when he arrived at the house, the auctioneer, who knew him fairly well, insisted that he should change into some dry clothes. He borrowed some trousers, socks and shoes from the foreman porter who was, however, a lean man while Way had what he described as 'a bow front'. Thus, the top four buttons of the trousers would not fasten. His only remedy was to cover his embarrassment with a long porter's coat, in which he then went off to view the sale.

Once inside the house he was taken for a porter and asked to provide measurements of a safe that was for sale. Using his ingenuity Way fished around in the voluminous pockets of the coat and produced a ruler with which he was able to provide the information. He was now in his element and continued to play the part, walking around the view and providing spontaneous, sometimes spurious information when interrogated. Eventually, he bumped into his friend, a Mr Hare of Taunton, who asked him what on earth he was doing. Way replied whimsically that as business had been so scarce recently, he had been forced into taking a part-time job.

The Sales

i Bidding

People are never so near playing the fool as when they think themselves wise.

Lady Mary Wortley Montagu
(Letter to the Countess of Bute)

Bidding at auction is one of life's great excitements from which many people shy away. 'Oh no!' they say, 'I might scratch my chin or sneeze at the wrong moment, and find myself with something I don't want.' In fact, bidding is usually extremely simple. The secret is to make sure that the auctioneer is clear about your intentions. Mistakes, however, do sometimes happen, particularly as the etiquette of the saleroom is often quite difficult for the newcomer to appreciate fully.

The father of a porter at Christie's King Street had arranged to meet his son to take him out to lunch. Unfortunately, there happened to be a sale on at the time and slow bidding meant that it was taking rather longer than expected. Having waited outside for half an hour, this impatient gentleman rushed into the saleroom and, waving to his son in desperation, immediately found himself the rather confused owner of an eighteenth-century picture.

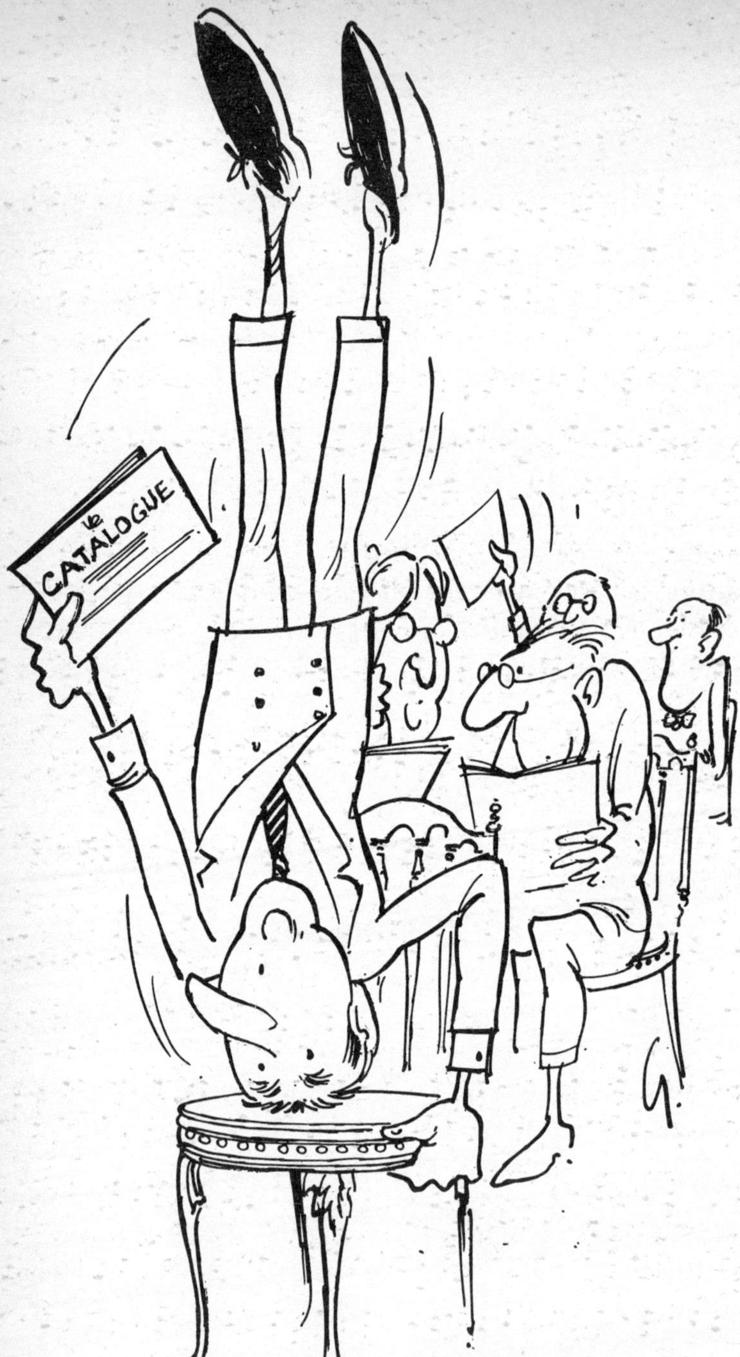
le CATALOGUE

Even the most experienced people can find themselves the owners of items for which they had no intention of bidding. On 22 June 1977, Sotheby's held an evening sale of Impressionist paintings from the Von Hirsch collection. Some way into the sale, a continental dealer momentarily forgot where he was and waved his blue entrance card at a friend who had just entered the saleroom. In so doing, he unsuspectingly bought a sculpture by Daumier for £3,600. (It was later re-sold at £3,900.)

A similar mistake occurred at a sale of fine French furniture at Parke Bernet of New York. A collector had made a specific agreement with the auctioneer — when this gentleman's coat was open he would be bidding, when it was buttoned he would have stopped bidding. This seemed a simple enough way of not attracting unwanted public attention. However, half-way through the sale, the collector, catching sight of a friend of his who was standing in the doorway, ran out with his coat flying around him. When he returned, it was to discover that he had bought a settee of particularly vulgar design for a quite enormous sum. (There is no record of his being able to re-sell it.)

As well as knowing how to bid, it is always wise to make sure that you know for what it is you are bidding.

A friend, a well-known dealer and collector of rare prints, relates the story of how, when he was just setting out on his life in 'the trade', he cleared out a vast pile of redundant, fourth-rate stock, mainly worthless reproductions, placing them in a London saleroom in one lot. On the day of the sale the dealer rang the auctioneers and enquired as to how he had done. When he learnt that his fourth-rate stock had realised a first-rate price his initial incredulity turned to joy and he rushed out and bought several bottles of champagne. As he was opening the first of these his partner entered, having returned from his daily foray into 'the market'. He, too, seemed pleased with himself, having acquired a bundle of useful prints for, as he put it, 'a pittance'. They drained their glasses, and as his partner opened a second bottle the dealer took a look at the newly acquired prints. He immediately dropped his glass – his partner had bought back their own redundant stock.

Circumstances were fairly typical for the sale of the contents of Auchinedin House by Christie's in May 1982. Many kinsmen of the Camerons who owned the house had flown across to Scotland from the United States in search of 'instant ancestors', thus ensuring a full saleroom and good prices.

The Camerons had decided that they wanted to retain some pieces which had been catalogued, but only if they were not fetching a high enough price. Rather than place on these items a 'reserve' price below which they would not be sold, they had decided to bid themselves, in this case permissible.

The auction proceeded and a highly fraught situation arose over one particular piece which Mr Cameron was attempting to wrest from the clutches of a bidder whom he was unable to see. As his agitation rose, so did the price offered, but still the piece was not his.

Eventually, the auctioneer inclined in his direction and said with a quiet smile:

'Mr Cameron, I think that I should inform you, that for the past few minutes you have been bidding against your wife.'

Perhaps one of the most notorious mix-ups over bidding occurred at a sale of Important Old Master Pictures held by Christie's on 19 March 1965, of which the main attraction was Rembrandt's *Portrait of his son Titus*.

The bidding gradually rose above the European auction record of £700,000 and was eventually narrowed down to a Los Angeles collector, Norton Simon, and Marlborough Fine Art, who had the bid at £740,000.

The auctioneer, Ivan Chance, glanced in Mr Simon's direction, to no avail, and the hammer fell: '£740,000 to Marlborough Fine Art.' Immediately Simon yelled out 'I bid,' and leaping from his chair, rushed to the rostrum where he grabbed a piece of paper from under Chance's nose and read aloud to the saleroom:

> When Mr Simon is sitting down he is bidding,
> When he stands up he has stopped bidding,
> If he sits down again he is not bidding until he raises his finger,
> Having raised his finger he is bidding until he stands up again.

The picture was put up again and bought by Simon, finger raised, for £760,000. The object of this highly complex agreement, however, had been completely defeated, and the Rembrandt was sold in a blaze of publicity.

We conclude this section with the tale of 'the bidder who never was'.

After an auction held at a Glasgow saleroom, the auctioneer, somewhat befuddled by his labours, was looking through the accounts to see how much each bidder had bought. He suddenly stopped and asked the clerk whereabouts in the room a certain Mr 'N.S.' had been sitting, as it seemed that he had bought a great many lots and it might be useful to recognise him in future. The clerk was barely able to keep a straight face. N.S. is the abbreviation used for those lots Not Sold.

ii Strange Sales

We have been able to dispose of
Rows and rows and rows of
Gainsboroughs, and Lawrences
Some sporting prints of Aunt Florence's
Some of which were rather rude . . .

Noel Coward,
The Stately Homes of England

The general impression of the auction house is of a place where one can either 'dispose of', or 'avail oneself of' fine pictures, furniture and works of art. However, there has always been, and one hopes always will be, a market for almost anything and some exceedingly strange things have in the past fallen under the hammer.

It is perhaps doubtful whether an auctioneer these days would have the courage to conduct such a sale as that referred to by Herodotus, at which Babylonian gentlemen were able to purchase their wives:

> The greatest beauty was put up, and knocked down to the highest bidder; then the next in the order of comeliness — and so on to the damsel who was equidistant between beauty and plainness, who was given away gratis. Then the least plain was put up, and knocked down to the gallant who would marry her for the smallest consideration — and so on till even the plainest was got rid of to some cynical worthy who decidedly preferred lucre to looks.
>
> Herodotus, *Cyrus*

After the auction the prices realised were totalled, and this divided equally among the vendors! One dare not imagine what turmoil such practice might cause today.

As far as we know, this means of procuring a partner became redundant long before the eighteenth century, although it was obviously fairly well-known, and occasionally even contemplated, as by a certain 'Mr Sarcastic'.

> I said to Miss Pennylove, whom I knew to be laying herself out for a good match,

LOT
201

'When my daughter becomes of marriageable age, I shall commission Christie to put her up at auction: the highest bidder to be the buyer; and if any dispute arise between two or more bidders, the lot to be put up again and resold.'

Thomas Love Peacock, *Melincourt*

Many other items of natural historical interest have also passed under the hammer.

From the 1830s, Henry Stevens's rooms in King Street, St James's, specialised in botany and zoology. At the sale of the Surrey Zoological Gardens in 1855, one could have bought an elephant for £336, or, for enthusiasts with a less well-lined pocket, a Pelican for £18 10s.

On one occasion a Great Dane was left overnight in the auction rooms prior to the sale. Unfortunately he managed to break loose from his tether, and when the porters opened the doors in the morning, he ran straight past them and out into the street. A great chase ensued along the length of King Street and through St James's, Belgravia and Chelsea, until eventually the canine giant was lost on the Embankment. The owner, on being informed of the loss of his property, promptly claimed £8 compensation, but a week later was amazed to find on opening the door of his house in Croydon to persistent scratching his dog, totally emaciated. Henry Stevens was so impressed with the intelligence and loyalty of this remarkable animal that he bought him, as a pet.

Stevens's also held sales of parrots. From their catalogue descriptions, all of them seem to have been blessed with a clean vocabulary, one particular bird being described as 'a young grey parrot, a matchless talker who does not know any bad language.' Not all, however, were very well versed in social niceties. One philanthropic old lady, who on viewing one of these birds waiting to be auctioned was heard to remark:

'Poor devil, he has nothing to eat.'

She was much taken aback when the parrot replied:

'What's that to you?'

Stevens's bird fanciers seemed to have fallen foul of their quarry on a number of occasions. During one sale it would seem that the entire audience was poking fun at one of the lots, a blackbird. The saleroom was filled with the sound of mocking laughter. This, however, soon became an incredulous hush when the blackbird opened its beak and let out a perfect imitation of its persecutors.

In his young days, Stevens held a sale of sea shells. Bidding was fairly restrained until a particularly rare shell came up, for which a previously unknown collector started to bid fiercely against the usual competition, eventually securing it for an outrageous sum. After the sale, but before the room had emptied, this gentleman collected his purchase from the porter and bore it to the foot of the rostrum. There, before the audience, he flung it to the floor, shattering it into a million pieces, at the same time declaring:

'Now I *still* have the unique specimen.'

One wonders how many times a successful bidder at one of Stevens's sales regretted his curious purchase. In the 1830s a Mr Conrad Cooke bought a monkey for a paltry sum, and was well pleased. However, when he got it home to his house in fashionable Clapham, it proved so mischievous that he was forced to tether it. Predictably it untied itself and, leaping out of a window, ran on to Clapham Common. Mr Cooke instinctively rushed after it, but eventually realised, from the size of his curious audience, the spectacle which he was making of himself and gave up the chase. Some time later, a great crowd of urchin boys appeared at his door, bearing the prodigal monkey aloft, and each demanding a pecuniary reward for its recovery. Mr Cooke thanked them all very much, took delivery of his purchase and without hesitation made a gift of the monkey to the London Zoo.

We should not leave Mr Stevens without noting that his final exit from the auction world was accomplished with a degree of the bizarre appropriate to his career as auctioneer of curious objects. When about to open a sale of orchids – his speciality – he collapsed and died on the rostrum.

Saleroom deaths such as Mr Stevens's are not a common occurrence but occasionally perilous situations do arise. In 1810, Christie's sold the contents of the house of Johan Zoffany, the celebrated portraitist. This sale should have been one of the successes of the season, being situated as it was at Brentford – in those days a charming little village. In normal circumstances, Christie could have counted on a large attendance for the sale which would have made a pleasant day's picnic in the country. He was sadly disappointed, however. The sale was a disaster and those who *did* attend were putting themselves in mortal danger – Zoffany had died of the plague.

It was not only Henry Stevens who sold animals. There have been country auctions of sheep, cattle, horses and all sorts of livestock since time immemorial. These are usually fairly straightforward affairs and very much a part of country life. Difficulties only tend to arise when the smart 'city' auctioneer attempts to dabble in such matters.

When, in the 1970s, the contents of Belvedere House, in Ireland, were auctioned, among them were found a number of peacocks. These were sold in mating pairs 'as viewed'. The notorious pride of the peacock must have been severely wounded by the

ignominy of being sold publicly, for when the successful bidders arrived to claim their prizes, the birds were nowhere to be seen. They were eventually found to have taken refuge high in the tallest trees on the estate, and no efforts on the part of the porters could dislodge them. Furthermore, the 'mating pairs' were now confused and exactly which lot was which was totally unclear. Not surprisingly, the buyers demanded a refund.

The luck of the Irish must help to explain the slightly more successful sale of peacocks which were among the contents of Ballyseedy Castle in County Kerry sold by Hamilton and Hamilton of Dublin. Once again the birds were sold in pairs, and once again they eluded all attempts by the porters to catch them, running around the castle grounds with loud screeches. The auctioneer Arthur Williams desperately tried to find a solution. He called in the local gamekeeper, who thoughtfully applied all the science of bird husbandry to his task — without success. Eventually, after hours of fruitless pursuit, Williams hit on a particularly Irish solution. He offered a couple of 'fivers' to those timeless inhabitants of the Irish landscape, the local tinkers. Within half an hour all of the peacocks were in custody, and, although maybe not in *precisely* their original lots, were safely delivered to their purchasers.

Over in Scotland, in the early 1980s, Christie's and Edmiston's of Glasgow held a charity auction in which two of the lots offered were a greyhound and a Shetland pony. The sale progressed and eventually the Shetland pony was announced, but did not appear. The auctioneer paused, and again called for the pony, but there was still no sign. The auctioneer began to look puzzled, and then a little uneasy as the audience started to giggle.

Meanwhile, somewhere in Glasgow's one-way system, the pony was travelling round and round in his horsebox. The ever diligent Strathclyde police had found him parked on a double yellow line and moved him on.

Animals of all varieties, and in every conceivable condition, seem on more than one occasion to have involved the local constabulary in the auction business.

In 1979, Christie's South Kensington held an important auction of natural history and sporting trophies, after which they received a polite, but characteristically succinct little note from the Metropolitan police, asking them to:

> . . . Notify us in good time in future before attempting further movement of elephant and gorilla through the streets of the Metropolis.

In transporting some of the specimens for sale from the Old Brompton Road to the Television Studios in Shepherd's Bush where they were to be filmed, Christie's had, for several hours, brought all of the traffic along this major route through London to a complete standstill.

Animals are by no means the strangest things to have been auctioned. In the 1970s, at a sale in the magnificent 'Sporting d'Hiver' at Monaco, Sotheby's offered a coat which had originally belonged to the Emperor Napoleon, and had been taken after Waterloo by the Prussian Field Marshall von Blucher.

The glittering saleroom was filled to capacity, largely, but not surprisingly, by French buyers, and the bidding was enthusiastic, eventually reaching 29,000 francs. The hammer fell and the auctioneer announced the name of the purchaser.

'His Grace the Duke of Wellington.'

An incredulous hush descended on the saleroom. After a moment's silence, an aggrieved French voice was heard from the back of the room:

'Mon Dieu, is he *still* alive?'

Clothes were also among the property of the Chevalier d'Eon de Beaumont, sold by James Christie in 1784. This gentleman had led a varied life. In France, Russia and England he had developed a reputation for dressing as both a man and a woman, as it suited his purpose. At the age of fourteen he enrolled in the French Army. Later in Russia he was one of Catherine the Great's most trusted ladies-in-waiting, and in London he emerged as a 'beau'. Eventually, the French government became so embarrassed by his political intrigues that they granted him a state pension on the condition he live out his life as a woman.

Chrsitie's sale catalogue whimsically described his property as:

> Consisting of the wardrobe of a Captain of Dragoons and a French Lady,

and carried the following bolderisation of Juvenal's satirical commentary on the female gladiators of his time:

> *Quale decus verum si Virginis Auctione fiat*
> *Balteus et Manical et Cristae crurisque sinistri*
> *Dimidium tegmen!*
> *Tu felix, Ocreas vendete Puella*

> A fine state of things if an auction should be held of your lady's gladiatorial properties; her belt, gauntlets, plumes . . . You will be a lucky fellow when the young woman sells her greaves (i.e. when she gives up the sport of the arena for that of the boudoir!).

In the mid 1970s Christie's held the first sales of historical steam engine models, quite a trend-setting departure at the time which elicited a good deal of publicity. This continued right up to the morning of the sale when Jonathan Minns, who had catalogued it for Christie's and was himself a major enthusiast, could be seen, looking like a boy with a new toy, driving a steam locomotive up and down King Street much to the amusement (and possibly envy) of passers-by.

There is even a group called the Ephemera Society which concerns itself solely with objects that others would normally consign to the dustbin. In 1976 these 'junk' enthusiasts held an auction in, of all places, a Hampshire rose garden. Among the lots were a broadsheet from 1843 advertising the services of a stallion, and a piece of wrapping paper from a grocer's shop *circa* 1910. The auctioneer was seated behind a card table, precariously balanced atop a kitchen table, in the shade of a yew tree, while the bidders were distributed about the garden, one even in the potting-shed. One of the lots was sold to a book dealer from Portobello who went unrecognised by the auctioneer since he was sitting behind some azaleas and was thus knocked down to 'the gentleman behind the bush'.

People have also attempted to auction:

'A cat with eight legs, two tales (sic), dog's head and cat's smellers which only lived fifteen minutes.'

'A cigar half smoked by his majesty, King Edward the Seventh.'

'A copy of a letter written by our Saviour Jesus Christ, and found eighteen miles from Icorium sixty-three years after the date of the Crucifixion, when it

was transmitted from the Holy City by a converted Jew, and translated from the original Hebrew.' (This letter allegedly contained the commandments of Christ and was signed by the Angel Gabriel!)

'A copy of King Agburus's letter to Christ, and his answer.'

'A hoof of the ass that our Saviour rode out Asia on.'

Chronologically these 'holy relics' lead us back to the Roman Empire which is where we started. In this, as in many fields, it is the Romans who emerge as the founders of that delightfully civilised pastime which we know today as the auction.

FINIS

The auctioneer sighed with joy,
The customary formalities
Were quickly over, and the strangers
Nodding a brief good-bye departed.

From The Auction Sale *by Henry Reed, 1958.*